Paths to Recreate

Own

LIFE!

Birister Sharma

Dedicated to my loving wife....

Pallabi Devi Sharma

I surrendered to you, O my Lord……

"Om Namah Shivaya"

Table of Contents

One Word

You're the builder of your own life. Everything depends on you. You can build your own life. You can ruin your own life. You can make your life like heaven. You can make your life like hell. You're responsible for your own growth. You're responsible for your own downfall. You're solely responsible for everything you do in your life.

If you want to build your life, then you must know yourself.

If you want to build your life, then you must know your worth.

If you want to build your life, then you must know your skills and talents.

If you want to build your life, then you must know your strengths and weaknesses.

If you want to build your life, then you must set clear aims and objectives.

If you want to build your life, then you must focus on your life.

If you want to build your life, then never fear anything in your life.

If you want to build your life, then you must prepare yourself to face every challenge that comes your way.

---***---

1. Your Skills

We all are born with our natural skills and talents. There is no one in this entire world who is born without his or her skills and talents. Almighty God has bestowed upon us our natural skills and talents right from our birth. He makes us special and unique.

But, unfortunately, many people don't know their own skills and talents; only a few people know their skills and talents. Out of one hundred percent of people, only one percent know their actual skills and talents. That is the reason why only a few percent of people become successful in their lives, while the rest remain unsuccessful throughout their entire lives. Another reason behind this is that many people know their skills and talents, but they never try to grow and develop them. They have a false notion that their skills and talents will work for them as they are. But they have forgotten that their skills and talents will only work for them when they polish them, when they sharpen them, and when they grow and develop them regularly, day in and night out.

A naturally occurring diamond is never used for making jewelry; it requires polishing and cutting; only then will it transform into different designs and models. It is a natural phenomenon that if anything is lying unused for a while, it will start to erode its utility very soon, and after some time, it will become useless. The same phenomenon happens with our skills and talents. For instance, if you keep a knife unused for a few weeks or a few months, you will see it lose its sharpness. What does it mean? It means that everything needs regular use because a knife is made to cut things.

If you're a right-handed person, then your right hand is stronger than your left hand. And if you're a left-handed person, then your left hand is stronger than your right hand.

Why?

It is an obvious reason that you use your right hand more than your left hand if you're a right-handed person and vice versa.

A ship is built to sail in the open and wide sea, but not to anchor at the seashore or in the harbor. If a ship doesn't sail in the sea for a few days or for a few months, it will sooner or later stop working.

A skillful and talented singer will soon lose the rhythm of his voice when he stops his regular singing practice.

A skillful and talented player will soon lose his form if he stops his regular practice.

In a similar way, whatever skills and talents you have within you are for your growth and development in your life. You have to use them. You have to practice them. You have to polish them. You have to prepare them. You have to sharpen them. You have to take advantage of them.

Your skills and talents are worthless if you keep them idle. Your skills and talents will only flourish if you sharpen them for your growth and development. You'll only progress and excel in your life with your skills and talents.

If you have skills and talents, then you have nothing to worry about in your life. You'll never starve in your life. You'll never wander off the path of your life. Your skills and talents will unlock every door to your success. Your skills and talents will make everything possible for you. Your skills and talents will attract your success and glory.

Your natural skills and talents will die if you keep them idle.

You're nothing without your skills and talents. Without skills and talents, you're just like waste material. Your life is meaningless and purposeless. You'll be out of the race in your life if you lack skills and talents.

It is only your skills and talents that make you productive and worthwhile in your life. You'll only get your identity through your skills and talents, not by your name.

You'll never get any job or service simply by giving your name, but with your special skills and talents.

When a person goes to seek a job in any company or firm, first of all, he will be asked to show his skills and talents.

Why? This is because a company or firm only runs on the skills and talents of the employees.

If you've skills and talents within you, then don't hide them, but exploit them and cherish them. Your skills and talents are your best friends. They always help you grow and develop in your life. Treat them well, as how you treat them will determine who you become in your life. The world doesn't need your name or the background of your family, but your special skills and talents. You'll only change and transform your life with your skills and talents.

Discover your natural skills and talents, polish them, and see the great difference in your life.

---***---

Anecdote

John, a woodcutter, worked for a company for five years but never got a raise. The company hired Bill, and within a year, he got a raise. This caused resentment in John, and he went to his boss to talk about it.

The boss said, "You are still cutting the same number of trees you were cutting five years ago. We are a result-oriented company and would be happy to give you a raise if your productivity goes up."

John went back, started hitting harder, and putting in longer hours, but he still wasn't able to cut more trees. He went back to his boss and told him his dilemma.

The boss told John to go talk to Bill. "Maybe there is something Bill knows that you and I don't."

John asked Bill how he managed to cut more trees.

Bill answered, "After every tree I cut, I take a break for two minutes and sharpen my axe. When was the last time you sharpened your axe?"

This question hit him like a bullet, and John got his answer.

---***---

2. Never Fear

Fear means... Forget Everything and Run

Face Everything and Rise

Fear makes you weak. Fear makes you sick. Fear makes you helpless. Fear sucks your strength, energy, and power. Fear paralyzes your mind, body, and soul.

You'll lose your self-belief.

You'll lose your self-confidence.

You'll lose your self-discipline.

You'll lose your self-reliance.

You'll never move ahead in your life if fear is always dwelling within you. Your life will become like stagnant water. You'll live your life in the whirlpool of confusion and dejection.

You'll die before your actual death if you always live in fear.

The more you fear, the more you become fearful. Fear will only chase you when you try to run away from it. But as you face your fear, it will run away from you.

The fear of failure is the biggest blunder of your life. Your fear is only in your mind, but not in you. Overcome your fear as soon as possible if you want to achieve something great in your life.

If you fear riding a bicycle, you'll never ride a bicycle.

If you fear riding a bike, you'll never ride a bike.

If you fear driving a car, you'll never drive a car.

A swimmer never learns to swim if he fears water. He has to dive into the water in order to learn to swim.

A firefighter never puts out burning things if he fears fire. He has to play with the blazing fire.

You'll never initiate anything in your life if you fear everything.

Everything becomes impossible for you.

You'll live a mediocre life.

You'll remain left behind on the path of your life.

You'll never discover your true potential in your entire life.

Your fear will block your growth and development. You'll become like a handicap; you can't do anything in your life; everything becomes impossible for you. Fear is a negative energy that blocks the flow of positive energy in your life. Your fear will dominate you day and night. Many skillful and talented people can't do well in their lives only because of their fears. They fear doing anything. They fear initiating anything. Before starting anything, they think about the outcomes; they focus more on their fears rather than their work. As a result, they witness failure in their lives.

Don't focus on your fears; focus only on your work.

If all the great scientists, discoverers, and inventors of this world had feared for their endeavors, this world couldn't have witnessed the great discoveries and inventions we see today. They focused more on their work than on their fears. They faced their fears. They conquered their fears.

If you conquer your fears, you can achieve everything in your life.

Your fears are natural. Don't run away from them. Stand like a giant rock before them. Take them as your challenge. Figure them out. Find out their reasons. Then face them and conquer them like a brave soldier. There is no fear in this entire world that rules you without your consent.

Don't try to run away from your fears; face them and conquer them like a brave soldier.

One day, the lord of death, Yumraj, summoned his servant, Malaria, to present himself at his court immediately.

Malaria instantly attended the court of the lord of death, Yumraj.

Malaria saluted Yumraj and asked the reason for the immediate summons.

"Malaria," Yumraj said, "you go to the Mritulog (the world of death) immediately and bring one hundred souls of humans to the Yumlog within a month."

"My lord," Malaria said politely, "at this point in time, there is no record of any human soul to bring to the Yumlog."

Yumraj looked into the eyes of Malaria with his blazing gaze.

"Is there any urgency, my lord?" Malaria asked, trembling.

"Yes," Yumraj replied in his thunderous voice. "There is an urgency to bring one hundred souls of humans to the Yumlog immediately."

And the very next day, Malaria came down to the Mritulog to bring one hundred souls of humans. Then Malaria started spreading his deadly disease in the Mritulog. Within a few days, Malaria concluded his assigned job and returned to the Yumlog while carrying one thousand souls of humans. When Malaria returned before the allotted period of time, Yumraj was very surprised.

"Malaria," Yumraj said, "What happened? You've come back so early. You didn't bring one hundred souls of humans?"

"No, my lord," Malaria said, "I have brought one thousand souls of humans."

"What? How?" Yumraj was very shocked.

"My lord, actually, I have killed one hundred humans by my disease as per your order, but I have no idea how nine hundred humans died."

"I am so sorry, my lord," Malaria said in a sad tone. "It's not my fault."

"It's all right, Malaria," Yumraj said. "It's not your fault, but it's their fears that killed them."

"You've done a great job," Yumraj applauded.

"Thank you, my lord," Malaria bowed.

What is the moral of the story?

The moral of the story is that it's only your fear that kills you before your actual death.

Your fear is a terrible disease that kills you every moment. You couldn't eat. You couldn't drink. You couldn't sleep. You couldn't relax. You couldn't think of anything; you couldn't do anything; you couldn't move anywhere. Your fear makes your life like hell.

It's only your fear that kills you before your actual death.

Love your fears. Enjoy your fears. When you face your fears, you'll never lose your life, but you'll discover the hidden mystery of triumph, and at the same time, you'll be able to conquer your fear forever.

Don't allow the seeds of fear to germinate in your mind, because once you allow them to grow in your mind, it'll definitely harm you in no time. It'll eat up your self-belief, self-confidence, self-discipline, and self-reliance.

Your fear is the only bridge between your success and failure. If you cross your fears and conquer them, you'll reach the course of your success and glory. On the other hand, if you fail to cross your fear and run away, you'll never reach the course of your success and glory.

Your fear is the only bridge between your success and failure.

This world is not for those who fear to do anything, but this world is for those who dare to do everything.

It's your fear that makes you a coward in your life, and there is no place for a coward in this world.

Be brave and live a life of a brave heart. Your fear is the enemy of your success and glory. Try to see opportunities in your fears rather than seeing your calamities.

Try to see opportunity in your fears rather than seeing your calamities.

It's only your fear that creates a hindrance in the path of your success.

You become a failure in your life because you fear your failure.

You can't live your life in fear.

You've to conquer your fear in order to make your life happy and prosperous.

You'll miss your golden opportunity if you live in fear.

Delete the word 'fear' from your dictionary.

Defeat your fear with your self-belief, self-confidence, self-discipline, and self-reliance.

Don't be the victim of fear.

Kill it before it kills you.

Your fears are nothing but self-created ghosts.

Only you can drive away your fear.

Anecdote

Two seeds lay side by side in the fertile soil.

The first seed said, "I want to grow! I want to send my roots deep into the soil beneath me and thrust my sprouts through the earth's crust above me…

"I want to unfurl my tender buds like banners to announce the arrival of spring…

"I want to feel the warmth of the sun on my face and the blessing of the morning dew on my petals!"

And so she grew…

The second seed said, "Hmmmmm… If I send my roots into the ground below, I don't know what I will encounter in the dark.

"If I push my way through the hard soil above me, I may damage my delicate sprouts…

"What if I let my buds open and a snail tries to eat them? And if I were to open my blossoms, a small child might pull me from the ground. No, it is much better for me to wait until it is safe."

And so she waited…

A yard hen scratching around in the early spring ground for food found the waiting seed and promptly ate it.

---***---

3. Build Your Life

Nobody can build your life better than you yourself. Nobody can force you to build anything without your consent. You're the builder of your own life. The way you are is the way you can build your life. Give your 100% effort in whatever you do in your life, whether you witness success or failure. Don't give up! Give your best in your life. Do your work as if it will be your last. Never do anything with a 50-50% mindset. Give your mind, body, and soul. Your life is not a fictional drama; you won't get another retake or another chance to amend your mistakes or errors. Your life is practical; there is no retake, and you will never get another chance.

Your life is a result of cause and effect. If the cause of your life is good, then its effect is always good, and finally, the outcome will follow the same.

When a potter makes a pot with mud, he tries to make it perfect because he knows that once a pot is allowed to dry in the sunlight, he wouldn't remake it if he finds anything wrong with it. He has to break his pot in order to remake it. The same case applies to your life.

Whatever you do in your life, always do it perfectly because you never know whether you'll get another chance to remake your life or not.

Try to build perfect things in your life right from today. Don't leave anything for tomorrow. Don't procrastinate anything in your life.

Always follow the path of excellence.

Don't follow the path of shortcut methods; you'll never reach anywhere in your life. You'll just wander and be lost on your path.

Build your life in such a manner that you feel proud of yourself.

Set your own examples of excellence and reach new heights of greatness.

Create and build your own land of wonders.

If the Mughal Empire's Shah Jahan hadn't built the magnificent monument 'Taj Mahal' in memory of his beloved wife, Mumtaz Mahal, today it wouldn't be one of the seven wonders of the world.

What do you want to build in your life?

A Perfect Life?

An Excellent Life?

A Magnificent Life?

Ask yourself, every second, every minute, every hour, every week, every month, every year, and every moment of your life.

You'll get your own answer.

Everything is in your hands; you can build a heaven as well as a hell in your life; after all, you're the builder of your own life.

---***---

Anecdote

An elderly carpenter was ready to retire. He told his employer, the contractor, of his plans to leave the house-building business and live a more leisurely life with his wife, enjoying his extended family. He would miss the paychecks, but he needed to retire. They could get by.

The contractor was sorry to see his good worker go and asked if he could build just one more house as a personal favor. The carpenter said yes, but in time it was easy to see

What a shock! What a shame!

If he had only known he was building his own house, he would have done it all so differently. Now he had to live in the home he had built none too well.

---***---

4. Your Burden

Life is short and very precious, so relax and enjoy.

Don't spend your life burdened by unwanted desires, anxieties, tensions, sorrows, hatreds, egos, jealousies, frustrations, and hopelessness.

The more you trap yourself in the nets of these burdens, the more you'll get trapped in them, and you won't free yourself.

Be like a bird. Fly free in the open sky. A bird can't fly in the open sky if its legs are tied with a heavy weight.

You too can't fly if you're tied down by the heavy burdens of life.

Learn to live your life fully and freely.

Your life is not always a bed of roses, but sometimes it is full of happiness, and sometimes it is full of sorrows. But you have to live your life on both occasions while accepting everything.

Forget your bad memories and bad days; only learn good morals, wisdom, and knowledge from them, and move on in your life.

Forget your past and move ahead freely with new hope and enthusiasm.

You'll get nothing from your past. Living in your past means you have imprisoned yourself in the burdens of anxieties, sorrows, and frustrations. A man of burden can't live happily and peacefully in his life. His life is like a ship that is about to sink at any moment. Remove whatever burdens you have kept in your mind, body, and soul. What is a burden? A burden is nothing but a weight that you keep unnecessarily in your life. A burden is always a burden, no matter whether it is a small burden or a big burden. You'll always encounter trouble. You've got to get rid of it as soon as possible before it creates big trouble for you. Nobody can remove the burdens of your life. Only you can remove them yourself.

Your burdens may be your personal burdens (emotions, love, compassion, expectations, and desires), family burdens (mother, father, spouse, son and daughter, siblings), and social burdens (position, respect, and endorsement). These are actually not a burden; they are your responsibilities. You have to follow and maintain these responsible burdens. You'll never run away from these burdens; you have to accept them warmly. However, while performing and maintaining these responsible burdens, don't forget to live your beautiful life.

Balance your life as well as your family life and social life. Whatever burden you have been carrying today in your life is only because of the imbalance in your lifestyle. Take some time to know yourself and enjoy your own company.

The burdens of your life occur when you fail to plan; when you fail to make good decisions; when you fail to assess yourself; when you fail to execute your plans; when you fail to prepare yourself; when you lack aims and objectives; when you forget the real meaning and purpose of your life; and when you take everything for granted.

Be responsible in your life. Don't take anything for granted. Do the things that are good for you and good for everyone.

You'll only eliminate the burdens of your life when you become responsible.

You'll never achieve anything in your life if you hold the burdens of anxieties, sorrows, hatreds, egos, jealousies, tensions, frustrations, and hopelessness. You'll only sail the boat of your life when you free yourself from these burdens; otherwise, sooner or later, you'll drown in the sea of your burdens. Fill your life with the bundles of love, happiness, joy, smiles, laughter, honesty, generosity, enthusiasm, and optimism.

---***---

Anecdote

A lecturer was giving a lecture to his students on stress management. He raised a glass of water and asked the audience, "How heavy do you think this glass of water is?" The students' answers ranged from 20 to 500 grams. "It doesn't matter what the absolute weight is. It depends on how long you hold it. "If I hold it for a minute, it is OK. "If I hold it for an hour, I will have an ache in my right arm. "If I hold it for a day, you will have to call an ambulance. "It is the exact same weight, but the longer I hold it, the heavier it becomes."

"If we carry our burdens all the time, sooner or later, we will not be able to carry on, the burden becoming increasingly heavier."

"What you have to do is put the glass down, rest for a while before holding it up."

We have to put down the burden periodically so that we can be refreshed and are able to carry on.

Whatever burdens you are carrying now on your shoulders, let them down for a moment if you can. Pick them up again later when you have rested...

Rest and relax.

Life is short; enjoy it!

Wisdom: **In the end, what matters most is how well you lived, loved, and learned to let go.**

---***---

5. Your Diamond

Your diamond is always within you. In fact, you're a diamond of yourself. You don't need to look after your diamond anywhere. Everything is right within you. You just need to awaken and arise yourself.

Almighty God has bestowed so much energy and power within you that you can do everything in your life; you can achieve everything in your life; you can build everything in your life; you can transform everything in your life.

You're born in this world not to become an ordinary man like a stone, a pebble, a tiny ant, or a tiny creature, but you're born to become an extraordinary man like a valuable diamond.

A diamond is a form of carbon, but under tremendous heat, energy, temperature, and pressure, it transforms into the hardest material: diamond.

You're like a diamond; when you don't receive the tremendous amount of heat, energy, temperature, and pressure—i.e., when you don't face and experience the tough struggles and challenges in your life—you wouldn't become tough and strong like a diamond.

You're like a priceless diamond. Know your worth and understand your purpose and mission in life.

You've got the same size brain that everybody has, but it is the caliber of how you use it for constructive and creative purposes in your life that matters. You're not measured by your body structure; you're measured by the power of your brain. Your brain is the master of your body, and your body is just a slave to your brain. Your body will follow you as your brain commands it. Use your brain in the right areas of your life and see the great difference it makes.

Your brain is the creator of your great thoughts, great ideas, great plans, and great decisions.

You'll only change and transform yourself when you've defined aims and objectives in your life. But if you don't have definite aims and objectives, you'll never change and transform yourself in your entire life. You'll wander in your life. Your life will become like a nomadic life, wandering hither and thither like a homeless creature.

It is only your definite aims and objectives that make you like a priceless diamond.

Why do some people become superior in their lives? And why do some people become inferior in their lives? Some people become superior in their lives only because of their skills and talents; they know how to utilize their potential in the right way. They concentrate only on their work rather than the outcomes. They know where to put their maximum efforts, energy, and power.

While some people become inferior in their lives, it is not because of a lack of skills and talents, but because they don't know how to utilize their potential in the right way. They concentrate only on the outcome rather than on their work. They don't know where to put their maximum capabilities.

If you have skills and talents, then nobody can defeat you on the battlefield of your life. It is your skills and talents that make you a valuable diamond in your life. You'll be a winner in your life if you know how to utilize your skills and talents. You can create your own opportunities if you know how to exploit your skills and talents in the right way and in the right direction. You can discover your own destiny if you know the right approach to using your skills and talents. You can construct your own road to success if you know how to direct your skills and talents.

Your skills and talents are the only tools that help you carve yourself into a priceless diamond.

What is barren land?

Barren land is land where there are no plants or trees. Its soil is infertile, full of stones, pebbles, and sand. There is no greenery; only dry and cracking soil spreads everywhere.

But when a hardworking farmer toils in it, and when he grows crops, plants, and trees, he transforms this same barren land into fertile and green land.

In the initial stage, your life is exactly like barren land, but as you toil and start nurturing and polishing your skills and talents in your chosen field, you enrich your growth and development and reap the fruits of wealth and prosperity. And you too become like a priceless diamond.

Many people fail to nurture and polish their skills and talents, so they cannot discover their hidden potential. They start looking for diamonds in the external world, but they have forgotten that the real diamond is always within them.

The real treasure is always within you.

Only you can discover it.

The real wealth is always within you.

Only you can discover it.

The real diamond is always within you.

Only you can discover it.

---***---

Anecdote

There was a farmer in Africa who was happy and content. He was happy because he was content. He was content because he was happy. One day, a wise man came to him and told him about the glory of diamonds and the power that goes along with them. The wise man said, "If you had a diamond the size of your thumb, you could have your own city. If you had a diamond the size of your fist, you could probably own your own country." And then he went away. That night, the farmer couldn't sleep. He was unhappy because he was discontent and discontent because he was unhappy.

The next morning, he made arrangements to sell off his farm, took care of his family, and went in search of diamonds. He looked all over Africa and couldn't find any. He looked all through Europe and couldn't find any. When he got to Spain, he was emotionally, physically, and financially broke. He became so disheartened that he threw himself into the Barcelona River and committed suicide.

Back home, the person who had bought his farm was watering the camels at a stream that ran through the farm. Across the stream, the rays of the morning sun hit a stone and made it sparkle like a rainbow. He thought it would look good on the mantelpiece. He picked up the stone and put it in the living room.

That afternoon, the wise man came and saw the stone sparkling. He asked, "Is Hafiz back?"

23

The new owner said, "No, why do you ask?"

The wise man said, "Because that is a diamond. I recognize one when I see one."

The man said, "No, that's just a stone I picked up from the stream. Come, I'll show you. There are many more."

They went and picked some samples and sent them for analysis. Sure enough, the stones were diamonds. They found that the farm was indeed covered with acres and acres of diamonds.

---***---

6. Focus

Focus on your goal.

Focus your mind, body, and soul only on your goal. You'll definitely achieve your success and glory in your life.

Don't allow your mind, body, and soul to distract for a microsecond from your goal.

It's only your focus that guides you to your ultimate destiny.

It's only your focus that helps you achieve your success and glory.

Without focus on your goal, you'll miss every golden opportunity in your life.

To pursue your chosen goal, you'll always come across many tough struggles and challenges in your life, and you have to make many sacrifices; but if you focus on your goal and are determined to reach your ultimate goal, then nothing will stop you, and nobody will dare to create any hurdles for you; you'll be able to tackle every hurricane of hurdles. You'll come out with flying colors at the end.

When you focus on your goal, you'll clearly see your success and glory. You can create a roadmap for your success. You'll know how to achieve your goal. You'll know how to reach your goal. You'll understand your struggles and challenges. You'll know how to build up your potential. You'll know how to prepare yourself. You'll get a complete assessment of your goal.

What things distract you from the goal of your life? Your wild desires, unwanted wishes, emotional feelings, idleness, procrastination, and instant gratification distract you from the goal of your life.

These are the biggest enemies of your goal. Once you defeat these enemies, you'll reach your goal. Keep yourself away from the sidelines of these biggest enemies of your goal.

Forget your wild desires. Forget your unwanted wishes. Forget your emotional feelings. Forget your idleness. Forget your procrastinations. And give up the joy of getting your instant gratifications.

Forget everything that distracts you from your goal. Only keep your focus on your goal until you reach it.

What is the biggest quality of a successful person?

The biggest quality of a successful person is his focus on his goal. He keeps himself aroused and awake; never sleeps or takes rest until he reaches his ultimate goal.

It is rightly said by **Swami Vivekananda:**

"Arise! Awake! And stop not until the goal is reached."

It's only your focus on your goal that makes you successful or unsuccessful in your life.

If you focus on your goal, even if you're slow, you'll definitely reach your goal.

Recall the old story of the tortoise and the hare.

The tortoise symbolizes a person who is focused and steadfast in his life, while the hare symbolizes a person who is distracted and idle.

Nobody can stop you from becoming successful in your life if you always focus on your goal.

Your focus is the only key to achieving your goal.

If you focus on your success, you'll become successful.

If you focus on your failure, you'll always witness failure in your life.

Your success always demands focus from you.

There is great energy and power in your focus.

When a piece of paper is put under a magnifying glass and placed in the sunlight, it catches fire.

What does it show?

It shows the energy and power of focus.

When you focus on anything, you'll become so full of energy and power that you can achieve anything in your life.

If you focus on your goal, then nobody can distract you from your chosen goal.

Focus is the energy and power of a winner.

Distraction is the only enemy of a winner.

Ask an archer if he couldn't focus on his target for a microsecond; what would happen to his target? He'll not only miss his shot but also be disqualified for the next round of the game.

When a hunter sets a target, he focuses on it in such a way that if a tiny fly, a small ant, or a small insect disturbs him, he remains cool and calm and stays in his position, standstill, until he shoots his target.

Focus on your goal like a hunter.

Focus on your goal in such a way that you'll forget everything.

Only focus on one goal at a time. Don't focus on too many goals at one time. When you focus on many goals at once, you'll become confused, distract yourself, and never reach your ultimate goal. A boatman couldn't sail two boats at one time. He can only sail one boat at a time. But if he ever tries to sail two boats at once, he'll just invite his own demise.

Don't focus on two things at one time.

Focus only on one thing at a time.

When you're traveling on a road and come across a crossroads where four roads intersect, if you don't know the exact road to your destination, you'll become confused and lost. But if you know the exact road to your destination, then you can move ahead.

Exactly the same thing would happen in your life. If you know your life's goal, then you'll definitely reach your life's goal no matter what happens.

If you want to enhance your life with a bunch of happiness, success, glory, peace, and prosperity, then only focus on your goal. Don't think of anything other than your goal. Just focus on your goal.

Set your goal, then focus on your goal; you'll always find your success and glory waiting for you.

Only focus on your goal!

Only focus on your goal!

Only focus on your goal!

Your focus is the only mantra for your success and glory.

---***---

Anecdote

Following a major marathon race recently, one of the top female participants was interviewed by a sports writer. He wanted to know, among other things, how she felt about a particular hill for which this race was noted. Her answer was very insightful. She responded that she had run in many races, all with hills and valleys to contend with, and that she really couldn't remember a particular hill during this race. She said, "Hills and valleys are part of every race. They are just part of getting from the beginning to the end. I focus on the finish, not on the hills and valleys. The course of the race leads to the finish. I focus on that—the finish."

Life is full of hills and valleys, some of which could cause us to want to quit along the way. It is during these times that we need to check our focus and remember that it needs to be on the finish, not the difficulties along the way.

---***---

7. Choices

Life is all about your choices. Your life always depends on your choices. In every situation of your life, whether good, bad, or worse, you've got to make your choices. You can't live your life without making choices. If you think that you won't make any choice in your life, let's see where your life will lead you. But if you think like that, then you'll surely make a mistake. Not making choices in your life is itself like making choices in your life.

Your one choice may change the entire course of your life. You've got to choose the right thing in your life because once you fail to choose the right one, you'll miss it forever. You've got to choose the things that are the most significant for you in your life. You've got to discard the things that are insignificant for you in your life.

Whatever you're today; whoever you're today, whether you're good or bad; whether you're successful or unsuccessful; whether you're happy or unhappy; whether you're rich or poor, is only because of the choices you make in your life.

You should never blame others for your wrong choices.

You're responsible for your own choices, whether right or wrong; whether good or bad.

Always make your choices wisely, cleverly, and intelligently.

Think practically before you make any choice in your life.

Judge and analyze before you make any choice in your life.

Don't hurry to make your choices. Take your own time to make your choices. It doesn't matter even if you delay in making your choices, but don't make wrong or bad choices. Since one right choice will build your life, and one wrong choice will ruin your life.

Don't make your choices emotionally and heartily. If you make your choices on the basis of emotional feelings, you'll always make mistakes. Because when you make choices with your emotional feelings, you'll think with your heart but not with your brain.

Make your choices from a practical point of view. Because when you make your choices practically, you'll know what to do and how to do it in your real life.

Don't make your choices under any pressure.

Don't make your choices blindly. Make sure that you're good enough to make your choices correctly. While making your choices, always open the eyes of your intelligent mind. Think of both pros and cons.

Before you make any choice in your life,

Think for yourself.

Before you make any choice in your life,

Judge yourself.

Before you make any choice in your life,

Plan for yourself.

Before you make any choice in your life,

Prepare yourself.

Once a rock climber fell down and his left hand was stuck between two huge rocks. He tried very hard to release his left hand, but in vain. He couldn't. The more he tried to release his left hand, the more it was stuck between the two rocks. He spent five days and five nights without food and water. He was almost dead. He had only one choice left, and that was to cut his left hand. Finally, he cut his left hand with his knife and released himself from there.

In your life, sometimes you have to make a difficult choice in order to save your life and to save your loved ones. At that time, you have to make choices that are the most significant for you.

You'll make better choices when you gain wisdom, knowledge, and experience in your life. Your choices are only yours. You have every right to make your choices. If you see a great opportunity before you, then don't hesitate to make your choice. Just grab it. One good choice makes a great difference in your life, and one bad choice can ruin your entire life. Be careful before you make any choice in your life. It is like a shooting bullet; once a bullet is released from the barrel of the gun, it won't come back. Before you make any choice in your life, think about the great mission in your life, whether it will lead you to the path of greatness or to the path of downfall. Ask yourself again and again until you come to your best conclusion.

When you make a good choice in your career, you'll prosper in your life. But if you make a bad choice in your career, you'll always find yourself struggling throughout your life.

Your good choice is the key to your success in life.

In every walk of your life, your good choice is of great significance. For instance, if you choose a good life partner, your life will become happy and prosperous; if you choose good friends, you'll never feel alone; if you choose a good job, you'll always feel content in your work.

There is great significance in your good choice.

Why did Mother Teresa choose to become a nun? She made a choice to bring a great difference to the lives of destitute people. She had a mission in her mind before she made the choice to become a nun.

Why did Mahatma Gandhi resign from his active law practice in South Africa?

Mahatma Gandhi made a choice to liberate his countrymen from colonial rule. He knew his mission before he made his choice to lead his countrymen.

Do you know the mission of your life? Do you know your choices about your life?

If not, then find out the mission of your life before you make any choices.

You must know your aims, objectives, and missions before you make any choices in your life.

If you don't know how to make good choices, you'll never know how to live your life. But if you know how to make good choices, then you'll know how to live your life.

Good choices make you good.

Great choices make you great.

Bad choices make you bad.

You'll make your life the way you make choices in your life.

You'll be known by the choices you make in your life.

---***---

Anecdote

In a remote forest, a pregnant deer is about to give birth to a baby. It finds a remote grass field nearby a river and slowly goes there, thinking it would be safe.

As she moves slowly, she experiences labor pains. At the same moment, dark clouds gather around that area, and lightning starts a forest fire.

Turning left, she sees a hunter who is aiming an arrow from a distance. As she tries to move to the right, she spots a hungry lion approaching her...

What can the pregnant deer do as she is already in labor?

What do you think will happen?

Will the deer survive?

Will it give birth to a fawn?

Will everything be burned by the forest fire?

That particular moment?

Can the deer go left? The hunter's arrow is pointing!

Can she go right? A hungry male lion is approaching!

Can she move up? A forest fire!

Can she move down? A fierce river?

Answer: She does nothing. She just focuses on giving birth to a new LIFE!

The sequence of events that happens in that fraction of a second (moment) is as follows:

In a spur of the moment, a lightning strike (it is already cloudy) blinds the eyes of the hunter. At that moment, he releases the arrow, missing and zipping past the deer. At that moment, the arrow hits and injures the lion badly. At that moment, it starts to rain heavily and puts out the forest fire. At the next moment, the deer gives birth to a healthy fawn.

---***---

8. Obstacles

The obstacle of life is very important for your growth and development. It is necessary for your life. Without it, your life is not possible. It is a part of your life. You've to accept it and face it; and you've to overcome it.

Make every obstacle a ladder for your growth and development. But don't make it an obstruction to your growth and development.

The obstacles of life make you strong and brave.

Don't be afraid to face the obstacles in your life. Welcome them with an open mind and heart. When you face your obstacles, only then will you find the right ways to lead your life. You'll discover your hidden power and strength.

A small plant only grows and develops into a big and strong tree when it faces the obstacles of drastic weather conditions. The more it resists the strong wind and storm, the stronger and tougher its roots become.

You'll only grow and develop when you face the obstacles of your life.

In Japan, after every few minutes, there is a shaking from an earthquake, but still, the Japanese people don't panic; they face the obstacle of earthquakes every minute, every hour, every day, every week, every month, and every year. They have built their houses to be earthquake durable, and there will be no chance of any damage even if a big earthquake occurs. They have learned how to tackle and handle the obstacles in their lives.

In the hilly areas and mountainous places, there is no possibility of agriculture, but people learn to do agriculture even in hilly and mountainous areas; they have developed a method of step farming. They have learned how to tackle and handle the obstacles of life.

It's only the obstacles in your life that teach you how to live your life.

Have you ever imagined why every mountaineer wants to climb the highest peak in the world despite the fact that he knows there are many obstacles ahead in his path? The mountaineer knows very well that if he overcomes the obstacles in his path, he will witness great success and glory.

Every obstacle brings you a bundle of joy, success, and glory in your life.

When Alexander the Great came to India to conquer the Indian rulers, he first invaded Porus, the Hindu king. However, when he marched ahead to attack Porus, he and his mighty soldiers came across huge mountains, deep valleys, and rivers in their paths where there were no ways and no passes. Alexander and his mighty soldiers found themselves entrapped between the huge mountains, deep valleys, and rivers.

The soldiers of Alexander stepped back and urged him to pull back. But Alexander was determined and firm; he asked his soldiers to cut down all the trees and fill up the deep valleys and rivers with trees to make a way through it. His soldiers did the same, marched ahead, and defeated whoever tried to resist him in his mission.

You have to attack your obstacles before they make you weak.

When you face the obstacles in your life, you'll know who you are; you'll know where you stand in your life. You can polish your skills and talents according to the situation. You'll know how to overcome the obstacles in your life.

It's only the obstacles in your life that will help you figure out your strong points and weak points. You'll know the real meaning and purpose of your life. You'll know the importance of your life.

Without obstacles, you'll never become great in your life.

Do you know how an ordinary man becomes an extraordinary man? It's only the obstacles of life that make an ordinary man into an extraordinary man. Mahatma Gandhi, Abraham Lincoln, Martin Luther King, Nelson Mandela, Mother Teresa, and Helen Keller, initially, they were all merely ordinary men and women, but they became great men and women only because of the obstacles they faced in their lives.

The more obstacles you face in your life, the more you become strong, mature, and experienced in your life.

Don't see the obstacles in your life as obstacles, but see them as your glorious opportunities.

When you face the obstacles in your life, you're helping yourself build the strong foundation of your life. Without obstacles, your life will become boring and meaningless. It's only obstacles that make your life exciting and adventurous. The obstacles in your life are nothing but the tasks or examinations of your life to check your worthiness and whether you're eligible to live in this world with your head held high.

If the captain of the ship doesn't face the obstacles of high tides and sea storms, he wouldn't be able to handle his ship during harsh weather conditions, and he could possibly drown his ship.

The captain of the ship, who knows how to handle his vessel during high tides and sea storms, can sail smoothly and anchor safely at the seashore.

You're the captain of your own life. You have to face the obstacles in your life all alone. Nobody will come to rescue you. You have to rescue yourself from the obstacles of life.

Don't expect that life is always fair to you. Life is full of obstacles. Life means obstacles. No life, no obstacles. Only a dead man has no obstacles. And one who overcomes the obstacles in his life will only get glimpses of his beautiful life.

What do you want in your life?

If you want to witness the glimpses of your beautiful life, then you've got to embrace the obstacles in your life.

A gold miner doesn't get the shining gold without digging the goldmine. The goldmine doesn't give its gold to the miner by itself. But the gold miner has to face obstacles to mine the gold.

An Olympic winner doesn't win a gold medal without facing the obstacles posed by his opponents.

You'll never get anything without facing the obstacles in your life.

You'll never run away from the obstacles of life. You've got to face them no matter what happens in your life. Your life is always surrounded by obstacles; you'll never escape from them. You've got to fight against them if you want to see yourself successful and victorious.

Your obstacles will never last long in your life if you know how to deal with them. But if you fail to deal with your obstacles, they'll always chase you. They'll make your life pitiable.

It's always in your hands how to perceive the obstacles in your life, whether you see an obstruction or an opportunity. If you see obstructions in your obstacles, then you'll never see the glorious moments in your life. But if you see opportunities in your obstacles, then you'll see the glorious moments in your life.

It's only you who can transform your obstacles into your fortunes.

There is a great opportunity in every obstacle.

Obstacles never make you weak,

But it'll make you stronger.

Obstacles never make you poor,

But it'll make you rich.

Obstacles never make you a failure,

But it'll make you successful.

Obstacles never make you a coward,

But it'll make you brave.

Obstacles never make you an ordinary man,

But it'll make you an extraordinary man.

---***---

Anecdote

In ancient times, a king had a boulder placed on a roadway. Then he hid himself and watched to see if anyone would remove the huge rock. Some of the king's wealthiest merchants and courtiers came by and simply walked around it. Many loudly blamed the king for not keeping the roads clear, but none did anything about getting the big stone out of the way. Then a peasant came along carrying a load of vegetables. On approaching the boulder, the peasant laid down his burden and tried to move the stone to the side of the road. After much pushing and straining, he finally succeeded. As the peasant picked up his load of vegetables, he noticed a purse lying in the road where the boulder had been.

The purse contained many gold coins and a note from the king indicating that the gold was for the person who removed the boulder from the roadway. The peasant learned what many others never understand: every obstacle presents an opportunity to improve one's condition.

---***---

9. Struggle

Are you afraid to struggle in your life? If you are, then you'll never achieve anything. But if you're ready to struggle, then you can achieve anything. The whole world will fall at your feet. No struggle, no success in your life.

Struggle is the core part of your life. Your life is not possible without struggle. You'll never achieve anything without it.

Today you can walk, sit, stand, and run only because you struggled during your childhood to take your first step.

Nothing is possible without struggle. Your struggle is the only key to your success and glory.

It's your sheer determination to struggle that leads you to your ultimate goal.

Every year, thousands of young aspirants set their feet in Mumbai to try their luck in the Bollywood industry to become actors and actresses. Why? Because they know that if they can struggle, no matter what comes in their way, they will succeed in their endeavors. They prepare themselves for whatever struggles come on their paths to success. They accept their struggles. And those who can struggle till the end will come out with flying colors in their desired pursuits.

Your struggle is the first stepping stone to your success and glory.

If you are determined to struggle in your life, then nobody can move you away from achieving your desired goal. You're bound to achieve your goal. But many of them give up in the middle of their struggles, and they fail to achieve their goal.

One day, a small boy complained to his father that he had to struggle a lot in order to get his seat on the school bus, so he requested his father to buy a car so that his father could drop him off at school.

"Son," the father said, "struggle is a part of life. Don't be afraid of the struggle. It is only struggle that makes you strong and tough in your life."

However, the boy couldn't listen to his father. Then the father bought a car. The boy was very happy and excited. He went to school by car every day.

One day, while he was going to school by car, he saw a schoolboy who was crippled; his legs were twisted, and he was walking on his twisted legs and two hands. But he was happy and excited while crossing the busy road.

The boy felt very sad and guilty. He realized how hard and tough it was for the crippled boy to reach his school every day. He struggled every day, but he had never complained about anything.

From the next day, the boy asked his father not to drop him by car. He went to school by the school bus as before.

The struggles of your life never make you weak and helpless; they make you stronger and more powerful.

Before you jump to accept any struggle in your life, which means in any of your chosen fields, you have to give your one hundred percent effort until you reach your ultimate goal.

If you know how to struggle in your life, you'll know how to survive in your life. Your struggle teaches you how to fight back and bounce back in your life.

It's the struggle of your life that makes you adamant about sticking to your chosen goal and mission. Everything is possible with struggle.

If you throw yourself into the swimming pool, you'll struggle to swim in the initial stage, but gradually you'll learn the tactics of swimming. Your life is like a big swimming pool. You've got to jump into it in order to learn the ups and downs of your life. Nature teaches us how to struggle in our lives. Every living creature has to struggle in order to survive in this world.

Struggle is the law of nature.

A tiny honeybee travels hundreds of miles to collect the nectar of flowers every day. It has to struggle every day, but it never gives up; it just does its work.

A deer has to struggle every day in order to survive in the jungle because it never knows when the lions and tigers will attack and devour it.

A small bird has to struggle every day in order to survive in the air because it doesn't know when the hunting eagle will catch it.

A tiny fish has to struggle every day in order to survive in the water because it doesn't know when the big fish will swallow it.

If you want to survive in this world, then you have to struggle because if you can struggle, then you can survive in this world. And one who can survive is the fittest, and only he can struggle in this world.

Don't be afraid to struggle in your life. You'll never die when you struggle in your life, but you'll discover your hidden talents.

If you struggle in your life, then don't be afraid of it, but greet it with your warm heart. Since it is only your struggle that teaches you how to manage your life; it is only your struggle that guides you on where you have to move ahead in your life.

If you ever struggle to get food, then you'll know the value of food, and you'll know how difficult it is to live without food.

If you ever struggle to get water, then you'll know the value of water, and you'll know how difficult it is to live without water.

If you ever struggle to get money, then you'll know the value of money, and you'll know how difficult it is to live without money.

If you ever struggle to get a good job, then you'll know the value of your job, and you'll know how difficult it is to live without a job.

If you ever struggle to get a house, then you'll know the value of your own house, and you'll know how difficult it is to live without one.

If you struggle to survive in this world, then you'll know the value of your life, and you'll know how to live your life.

It is the struggle of your life that makes you realize the value of your life.

You'll never become a hero in your life without struggle. Every hero is the by-product of thousands of struggles. Without struggle, nobody becomes a hero in real life.

Champions are never born overnight; they are made through struggle in their lives. Olympic champions have to struggle for many years, at least seven to eight years; they have to go through tight and rigorous practices and training sessions day in and day out before they finally qualify for the Olympic Games.

Your struggle is very significant for you to move ahead in your life.

Never indulge in self-pity. Never make excuses in your life. Come out of your comfort zone. Break the shackles of your weaknesses and build up the power of your strengths to move forward in your life. You'll never get anything for free in this world. You have to pay something in order to get anything in return. You have to struggle to achieve anything in this world. This is the law of this world.

Naturally occurring gold has no shine; it is dull, but when the same gold is melted in the fire, it gains its golden shine.

The same thing will happen to you; until you struggle in your life, you'll never shine. If you want to shine in your life, then don't be afraid to struggle.

When a small grain of sand falls into the sea shell, it doesn't know where it'll fall; in fact, it doesn't know its ultimate fate. It gets trapped inside the sea shell. It struggles to free itself, but in vain. And its struggle goes on and on continuously for many days, many weeks, many months, and many years, and ultimately it turns into a shining pearl.

Has not a small grain of sand struggled inside the sea shell, it couldn't turn into a valuable pearl.

This world is like the sea shell, and you're like a small grain of sand. When you set out on your journey of life in this world, you'll fall into the world of the sea shell. You'll get trapped inside it. You've to struggle all alone. Nobody will come to your rescue. And when you're able to struggle in this world, you'll turn into a priceless pearl.

Accept every struggle that knocks on your life, and give your best effort to beat it, and then see the great difference in your life.

---***---

Anecdote

A man found a cocoon of a butterfly. One day, a small opening appeared; he sat and watched the butterfly for several hours as it struggled to force its body through that little hole. Then it seemed to stop making any progress. It appeared as if it had gotten as far as it could and could go no further.

Then the man decided to help the butterfly, so he took a pair of scissors and snipped off the remaining bit of the cocoon. The butterfly then emerged easily. But it had a swollen body and small, shriveled wings.

The man continued to watch the butterfly because he expected that, at any moment, the wings would enlarge and expand to be able to support the body, which would contract in time. Neither happened! In fact, the butterfly spent the rest of its life crawling around with a swollen body and shriveled wings. It was never able to fly.

What the man in his kindness and haste did not understand was that the restricting cocoon and the struggle required for the butterfly to get through the tiny opening were nature's way of forcing fluid from the body of the butterfly into its wings so that it would be ready for flight once it achieved its freedom from the cocoon. Sometimes struggles are exactly what we need in our lives. If nature allowed us to go through our lives without any obstacles, it would cripple us. We would not be as strong as we could have been. And we could never fly....

---***---

10. Your Worth

You're born with great meaning and worth. Almighty God has blessed you with great worth. If you fail to know your worth, then you'll never do anything in your life. Your life will become meaningless and purposeless.

Figure out your worth. You'll definitely discover your values and strengths that are hidden within you.

If you have some flaws or weaknesses, you still have worth within you. Never underestimate your worth. Sometimes, your flaws or weaknesses can also become your greatest worth if you do something worthwhile in your life.

A stone is merely a stone if it remains unused, but when you strike it with another stone, it produces a spark of fire.

In a similar fashion, if you don't use your skills and talents properly for your progress, you'll never know your actual worth.

Don't be afraid of your flaws and weaknesses, but try to see worth in them. You'll definitely get an opportunity to correct your flaws and weaknesses.

One day, a young boy went to the Kung Fu Master in order to learn the art of Kung Fu. The young boy requested the Kung Fu Master to teach him all the tactics of Kung Fu. However, the Kung Fu Master noticed that the right hand of the young boy was weak. The Kung Fu Master didn't disclose anything to the young boy; he just turned down the request to teach him Kung Fu. The young boy bowed down and requested the Kung Fu Master many times to teach him Kung Fu. Finally, the Kung Fu Master decided to teach the young boy Kung Fu.

Then, from the next day, the Kung Fu Master started teaching the young boy Kung Fu. The boy was very happy and thrilled to learn the art of Kung Fu.

Many months passed, and the Kung Fu Master trained the young boy to fight with his left hand only. Then, one day, the young boy asked the Kung Fu Master about the reason for this. However, the Kung Fu Master didn't tell him anything and just told him to wait for the right moment.

After one year, the Kung Fu fighting competition was held in the town. Many trained Kung Fu fighters from far-off places were taking part in that competition.

The Kung Fu Master asked the young boy to take part in that competition. Initially, the young boy hesitated to take part in it. But the Kung Fu Master told him not to worry about anything and assured him that he was perfectly trained and that nobody could defeat him in Kung Fu.

The competition of Kung Fu began, and the young boy defeated all the competitors very easily, becoming victorious.

The next day, the young boy asked the Kung Fu Master about the reason for his victory. The Kung Fu Master then told him everything.

"On the very first day you came to me to learn Kung Fu, I noticed that your right hand was weak. I had decided not to teach you Kung Fu, but you requested me again and again. Finally, I decided to teach you only with your left hand. During the course of your Kung Fu training, your left hand has become so strong and powerful that you can defeat anybody in Kung Fu. You have become a master in Kung Fu."

The young boy was elated and touched the feet of his Kung Fu Master.

Nobody is perfect in this world.

If you're not perfect in your life, it doesn't mean that you're worthless or an outcast from this world. You have every right to make yourself perfect and worthy. This is your birthright, and nobody can snatch it from you.

When a piece of land is used for growing crops again and again, year after year, its fertility will be maintained, and at the same time, the worth of the land will increase further. However, when the same piece of land has been allowed to be abandoned for many years, its fertility will perish, and its worth will degrade as time passes.

The same thing will happen to you; as long as you work for your growth and development in your chosen field, your skills and talents will enrich, and your worth will increase further.

It is always up to you what you really want to become in your life.

You'll shine more in your life if you do something great and amazing, even if you have flaws and weaknesses. The players of the Paralympic Games are all handicapped, but they compete with each other like normal players, despite having flaws and weaknesses. They know where their worth is applicable to them. If you know where to apply your worth, then you'll be able to achieve anything in your life. If you discover your hidden skills and talents, then you'll know how valuable you are.

**Don't feel ashamed of your flaws and weaknesses, but try
to correct and amend them for your growth and development
and for the greater good.**

One day, a poor man visited the Swami and said, "Swamiji, I am
very poor. I have no house to live in. I have no work to do. I have
nothing. I am helpless. I am spending my life begging. I am the
poorest man in this world."

The Swami smiled and said, "Why? You have two eyes. You
have two ears. You have two hands. You have two legs. With your
two eyes, you can see this beautiful world. With your two ears, you
can listen to good things. With your two hands, you can do good
deeds for yourself. And with your two legs, you can travel anywhere
in this world. I see you as the richest man in this world."

The poor man got enlightenment, touched the Swami's feet,
and set out to begin his new life.

Every tiny little thing has some worth to contribute to this
world.

It's a well-known fact that if the bees become extinct or
disappear from this world, then the entire environment will be
affected.

Let's look at your own body parts; can you see any part that is
worthless?

No. Every part of your body is important for you, whether it is
your little fingers or the little hair on your body. Every part of your
body has a vital role in keeping you alive.

**Don't forget that you're born as a human being, the
strongest being on this earth.**

You can do anything in this world.

What are your values? Have you ever asked yourself? What you can do, nobody can do like you. What you can think, nobody can think like you. You're unique in this world. You're born with many special qualities of which you're not aware. You've got to discover them yourself.

Why do some people become very famous and well-known?

The only reason behind this is that they know their actual worth. They know in which areas they are good enough to move further in their lives. They act according to their worth, and ultimately they achieve what they really want to do in their lives.

William Shakespeare, the famous English author and dramatist; Albert Einstein, the famous scientist; Thomas Alva Edison, the famous inventor of the electric bulb; Michael Jackson, the famous pop singer of all time; Pelé, the greatest football player; Lata Mangeshkar, the famous playback singer of Bollywood; Amitabh Bachchan, the megastar of Bollywood; and Sachin Tendulkar, the God of Cricket, all became successful in their respective fields because they knew their actual worth and understood in which field they were best suited.

If you want to achieve something great in your life, then first of all, you have to know your actual worth.

If you think well, you can become a good thinker or a good philosopher.

If you can speak well, you can become a good speaker or a good orator.

If you can write well, you can become a good writer.

If you can sing well, you can become a good singer.

If you can compose well, you can become a good composer.

If you can dance well, you can become a good dancer.

If you can act well, you can become a good actor.

If you can paint well, you can become a good artist.

If you can play well, you can become a good player.

If you can manage something well, you can become a good manager.

And so on and so forth.

You have a storehouse of skills and talents within you; you have to discover them. Your worth will only grow and develop when you polish your skills and talents every day and every moment. But if you stay idle in your life, you'll never discover your worth, and nobody will ever help you to discover it. You have to discover it yourself.

You're not born in this world only to eat, drink, and sleep, and then one day die, worthless like ants and mosquitoes; you're born in this world to do something great in your life. Know your worth and rule this world.

---***---

Anecdote

A water bearer had two large pots, each hung on each end of a pole that he carried across his neck. One of the pots had a crack in it, and while the other pot was perfect and always delivered a full portion of water at the end of the long walk from the stream to the master's house, the cracked pot arrived only half full.

For a full two years, this went on daily, with the bearer delivering only one and a half pots full of water to his master's house. Of course, the perfect pot was proud of its accomplishments.

But the poor cracked pot was ashamed of its own imperfection and miserable that it was able to accomplish only half of what it had been made to do. After two years of what it perceived to be a bitter failure, it spoke to the water bearer one day by the stream.

"I am ashamed of myself, and I want to apologize to you."

"Why?" asked the bearer. "What are you ashamed of?"

"I have been able to deliver only half my load because this crack in my side causes water to leak out all the way back to your master's house. Because of my flaws, you have to do all of this work, and you don't get full value from your efforts," the pot said.

The water bearer felt sorry for the old cracked pot, and in his compassion, he said, "As we return to the master's house, I want you to especially notice the beautiful flowers along the path."

Indeed, as they went up the hill, the old cracked pot noticed the sun warming the beautiful wildflowers on the side of the path. But at the end of the trail, it still felt bad because it had leaked out half its load, and so again the pot apologized to the bearer for its failure.

The bearer said to the pot, "Did you notice that there were flowers only on your side of the path, but not on the other pot's side? That's because I have taken advantage of your flaw. I planted flower seeds on your side of the path, and every day while we walk back from the stream, you've watered them. For two years, I have been able to pick these beautiful flowers to decorate my master's table.

Without you being just the way you are and without your help, he would not have this beauty to grace his house."

56

---***---

---***---

About the author:

Birister Sharma is a full time author. He is also an avid reader. He loves reading, writing, and motivation. He has penned down dozens of self-help motivational books and novels so far.

You may contact him @ birister2007@gmail.com